# TYRANNUS NIX?

## FERLINGHETTI

To

Pressley E Bisland

father emeritus

## Books by Lawrence Ferlinghetti

A Coney Island of the Mind

After the Cries of the Birds

Her

Moscow in the Wilderness,
    Segovia in the Snow

Pictures of the Gone World

Routines

Starting from San Francisco

The Secret Meaning of Things

Tyrannus Nix?

Unfair Arguments with Existence

# TYRANNUS NIX?

## FERLINGHETTI

Nixon Nixon bush league President this is a populist hymn to you and yours And I begin with your face and come back to your face For 'our history is noble and tragic like the mask of a tyrant' And the mask an actor wears is apt to become his face

1

Nixon Nixon I saw your childhood home on TV
I saw your childhood face It was the same
face ~~the face of~~ adult America the face we
chose ~~for~~ America the space-race face ~~the~~
race face ~~the face that~~ sunk a thousand
sampans ~~the face~~ we all love in the Geritol
ads the face of the nation facing the nation

on color TV  the electronic burner that replaced
the log fire  the electric log  the gas log in color
with antenna up the chimney We sit entranced
by the burning images on the grid in the bright
grate the flickering faces in the crucible whose
light-intensity we can turn up to suit whose ver=
tical image we can adjust so that the lower half

3

of your face matches the upper half of your
face  What a groovy invention Just what we
needed old Blunderbuss Face old Circuit
Preacher face American Gothic Bold Face
with italic lips on the teleprinter  I've got to
hand it to you Old Family Friend your face
hasn't fallen apart yet like some of your

liberal Presidential opponents the slack lips and
fallen chins betraying the higher ideals of the fine
brow You've held it together somehow after your
own fashion or at least you put it back together
in private Americans love underdogs and your
jowls growled Old Lionhearted but your eyes kept
their curious focus You beamed them on the fences

You aimed at the top bleachers and swung and swung and swung and finally connected with the sandbags loaded You're off and running And the ball is lost in the sun

Nixon oh Nixon will anyone catch it Where will it come down Fair or foul The Dodgers may win this year in the draft The winds are extra strong in this park A lot of old hands are ready to hang up their cleats we hope This is one national sport we hope is on the way out The Whither White Sox we hope are all washed up It's time for a new umpire and a new Hall of Fame Throw out a new ball and a new uniform

and a new flag too while you're at it and make
the flag green this time instead of bloody red
and black-and-blue The national spectator sport
shows more and more dark faces on TV They
can run faster and hit harder than anyone
and there's millions of them where they came
from over there and they all look alike You're

8

hungry an hour after you eat one  Here they
come   Blow their heads off   You may be live
on TV Telestar   Zap those Gooks

Nixon Nixon  I'm singing you this baseball Diamond
Sutra from way out here in New Left Field in the
International League   I'm keeping up the chatter

as if we had to back you up for some strange reason
Aren't you actually as homey and honest as Uncle Ezra
Aren't you really the good guy at the fillingstation all my rela-
tives voted for  Aren't you to be trusted after all these
years during which nobody really trusted you  Aren't you
just the man to buy a used war from  Is there a
tiger in the tank  You'd tell us if it really was

10

a bummer You'd tell us if the automatic transmission was shot You'd tell me if the tires were really retreads You'd tell us if the warranty was phony You'd not let us run out of gas a mile from the dealer would you Tiger

Nixon Nixon now that your team's taken the

11

field things are really tightening up out here And there's no relief in sight for you or us although it occurs to me that we are your relief if you'd only admit it Mister we've been warming up in the bullpen for a long time I'd love to be your catcher for a while so I could send you some secret signals Will you make some sign if you can read

me But I never saw a pitcher with a mask
before What've you got under it That's what I've
been trying to fathom ever since they brought you up
from the minors Did you learn that windup with the
WhittierQuakers It's the most deceptive ever seen
in a World Series a windup that gives away nothing
and telegraphs nothing so that nobody still knows whats

coming We hope not a fast change-up  One wild pitch
and you've blown it    Your windup is so weird

Richard Poor Richard this is your Almanach de Gol-
gotha and we're your Cross   Is it true you once
went to a shrink to find out who you really were   I
hope so   It doesn't mean you're Sick   It means

you just recognized the onionskin of fucked-up
modern manunkind   Is it possible the New Nix
now is not really the same old Nix   Is it possible
for an old snake to learn new tricks   Between election
and inauguration you seemed somehow to make an
invisible effort to slough off the old snakeskin
But the pattern of the old slippery scales keeps coming

through as you still manage to slither around the bases touching all of them at once and there are still at least twenty of them    Slide Kelly slide

Richie oh Richie   I seem to be developing a real fondness for you in spite of your spots Do you love me   How I'd love to be cheek-by-jowl

with you Old Buddy How I'd love to get you in my
encounter group and discuss inner space with you
and find out what's behind that hogjaw jughead
mask We land on the moon's inscrutable face
while yours is just as inscrutable Maybe you're part
Oriental maybe we could discuss Far out Eastern
arts or poetry Who's your favorite poet John

Greenleaf Whittier I am thinking maybe it's actually possible to communicate with you Wouldn't that be an unexpected development I am thinking maybe it's not too late and not too early and I'm naively curious why you can't just Declare Peace You can do it if Allen Ginsberg can and you can make it stick Old Sticky Dick You could have grabbed the mike right after Inauguration and blurted it out right there and then   I hereby declare the end of the War Against Youth.  Think what a hero you'd be with People or do you think people are a danger to the public Whereas they are probably only trans-ceiver mechanisms from some god  It occurs to me Old Tricky Dick that it's probably still ye Old Red menace that's stopping you Probably only someone fiddling with his moustache in a hopeless cellar

O Nixon Nixon when you or your ghost announced that the American Dream doesn't come to those who are asleep I stayed up all night to see what or who would come Some blue-velvet eternity or Magic Spring 1970 or maybe only West Point

New York  the American Daymare in all its glory
American Wet Dream over you  And us 'riders
on the earth together' above which our own
Roman Emperors of Space are about to have to
signal the end of the Christian era by finally prov-
ing your Dear God existeth nowhere at all up there
God's long nose still not in sight anywhere up there

21

and the only god of life on earth is consciousness itself
And love the Fourth Position in the whispered
hush of dawn in endless fields of light

Nixon o Nixon I dreamt of myself curled up
upon a big bed in the same position as my dog Head
tucked under tail sleeping and hiding from You I don't know

why exactly I'm telling you all this except that the curled-up image of self and dog is perhaps the image of paranoid America itself  The Vietnam albatross still hanging heavy 'round your neck oh Uncle Ahab and other overweight albatrosses still caught in the rigging of your ship still voyaging continually abroad in search of monsters to destroy Great White

Whales turning Red in the international waters of
paranoia where our free yellow submarine can't
reach you and you may lose your life like Ahab
in strange China Seas if you don't ever ever
see 'We're all one and life flows on within you
and without you'
Nixon ah Nixon I got the talking blues

24

I think I'll sing the Green Flag Rag rather than the
Blood Spangled Banner in the dawn's early blight
Do housewives dream of you  Are you sexy How's
your rig  Who can tell and it's irrelevant anyway
except except for what you might do by way
of sublimation  Our fate depends upon which one
of your fingers itches  And thy hand is fire

Nixon Nixon enigma Nixon your nowhere eyes
tell the true story of America and a picture
of them is worth a thousand false words Are
you 'a real man or a real machine with computer-
brain' Are you the fifty-five-year-old virgin
or are you Machiavelli smiling   I think you've
still got that infectious Pink Eye you caught on

the Unamerican Committee what with your yahoo
cohorts now conducting the nazification of California
and other campuses   I heard you plainly tell
them on TV to get a little tougher to get a little
rougher on campus and the next day they
murdered one of us to show how tough Thank
you Tyrannus Nix Let him be laid at your door

27

You waved your soft white hand and the trigger
moved unknown to you yet it moved down
the toilet chain of command  The Blue Meanies
are your real army oh my Commander-in-chief
Nixon! Nixon! The Revolution is coming The
TV is burning  Its one-eyed imbecile head is winking with

terror  They're using the same footage for the
War as for the Soap Opera with the same sponsor
The Third World is still coming at us over the
hill  You don't need spy planes + ships to see it
You need a Third Eye in the middle of your fore-
head  You've got one and don't know it
There's a mystic eye in the detached top of the

pyramid on the reverse side of the American dollar
on the reverse side of the Great Seal of the United States
It occurs to me the distance between the detached eye
and the broad base of the Establishment is the Generation Gap itself   You don't have a clue how to use
that Eye  and maybe even think you're supposed
to watch us with it like Big Brother through our

TVs down here in the dollar's green desert
It occurs to me it is also watching you Old Nix
It occurs to me it also sees a minotaur at the
heart of that labyrinth which is the Pentagon while
outside its eyeless walls citizens without hats
wind their white string as Buddhists burn
And the air is shaken with light

Nix oh Nix this morning by the Third Street Bridge
on the San Francisco waterfront I saw a black ship loading
barbed wire for Vietnam The huge rolls of it lay on deck
with Army tags attached By night they were rolling over the
sea Do Quakers love all sentient beings What kind of weird
Quacker are you anyway Like on the Quaker Oats Box
Don't rock the Mayflower Don't wear sandals

32

Avoid scandal  Batter's up and pole me a homer into
the Right field daisies   Only you run for me I'm
too old for all that  Have a good trip my son and
we'll vote for you   πTy son !  πTy son !

Nixon Nixon burning bright in the forest of our night
Did he who dug the Lamb dig thee  And will the Lamb follow

you What the ball what the chain In what freezer was thy
brain  I am trying to figure out what if anything makes
it tick and turn over or on  I am not saying you have
the mask of a tyrant  It is not anything but a huge question-
mark at this point  I know your hometown was run
over by a freeway like the lost hometown of every American transplanted heart  I got

34

lost on the cloverleaf and never found it but I
know it actually exists   It's the state of mind
of America made of six supermarkets four drive-
ins sixteen fillingstations and a college where
they taught what you learned   Quakers don't
believe in quakes   'Frozen soul of America
who will cling to the wreckage?'

Nixon oh Nixon the leaves are green in Whittier today but as every poet who has just discovered the word ecology will tell you DDT is killing the pelicans and their eco-system is our own Hudson River related to Hunters Point and Colorado River emptied into Vietcong Delta Zap those spooks and niggers won't win

Nixon Nixon Black Power's at bat and I sit in
the white bleachers eating crackerjack and reading
the whole newspaper column by column trying to
discover where you're really at  A hero with a
thousand faces none of which fit  Every head
has got you in it now Old Swivelhead  I read the
stories and find out nothing Eisenhoover is dead

and Nixon Sails Alone Around the World Nixon
says this and Nix says that but what as usual
does he himself believe if anything Will he grant
the Serpent free speech Freedom is no break-
fast food and Concentration Camp USA is not a
poetic image Though this psalm be
fraught with freedom

Nixon sweet Nixon have you had any sweet dreams lately Have you had your five dreams per night Have you ever looked them up in Freud to find out whose end is up Or do you prefer astrology which enables us to believe the fault is not in ourselves but in our stars It occurs to me if you had any mystic tendencies you'd probably go for Gurdjieff _Ayn Rand

and Scientology or some other psychic authoritarianism
Let us eat light   But a cock's cry doesn't open
the sun   You're probably full of hostilities behind that
Ed Sullivan smile   And how come your face reminds me
of the face of a pickpocket who meets a saint and sees
only pockets   And how come your face reminds
me of the face of a man who picks you up hitch-hiking

in a sunny central spot and lets you off out in the desert at night  How come there seems to be a No Man's Land and a No Woman's Land between thee and us on TV and how come you can't ever speak for yourself without reading it  When I took my orals I had to  But maybe Quaker Plain Speech ain't so easy as all that  I finally begin to realize you are

a very strange man Mister Jones   Not too strange
I hope    Like when you announce 'We only warn once'
It's a bit too bad you don't know how to dig those
bumperstickers 'Flying saucers are real The
Air Force doesn't exist' and 'We are the
people our parents warned us against' oh
Are we lost in our Sun Ra boat?

Nixon Nixon  I keep cutting back to your face as if
it's all we've got to go on  Mon Général once said
in a Kennedy he saw the smiling mask of America but
in Colonel Cornpone Johnson he saw the raw face
of America itself  And  I am thinking Old Slick Dick
in you we finally see no face at all behind the
great Seal of the United States  We see an index of

43

night The poets in their sad likenesses can't help you
Deadeye Dick but if you want "to open the door to a
room with a lot of other doors" why don't you open
the Doors of Perception You've got a free airplane
I want you to take a little free trip a little
trip with Alice I'll lend you my cabin in Big
Sur and you can sleep out under the pulsars

meditating Answers   It's too bad you're not 'addicted
to that inner place'  Have you ever tried the full lotus
position   I can't do it either but you'll have to take
off your establishment shoes to try it   You're not much
older than I  but about five generations apart
Why is it Presidents have to be flying mummies
in dying trajectories who never could make it

at the Fillmore Auditorium or Zen Mountain Center
I'm not ready to join you daddy with your honorary
membership in the FBI   Oh the vast sad camp which
is Washington
Nixon oh Nixon   Joy begat Joy and Love Begat
Love and Hate begat Hate and these are
the strophes and anti-strophes of ecstasy and

despair in this strange eclogue to you  But I'll not
be your Virgil heralding you a modern Emperor Augustus
who recognized the Empire's natural limits and
forthwith withdrew all armies overseas pronto thus
bringing the Age of Iron to a clanging close Oh Daddy
you're a legionnaire on the wall of the farthest reaches
of Empire looking out at the Darkness and not recognizing

47

the limits  One would think the wind still whispered latin phrases when whoever wrote our dollar bill took its not-so-mystic motto from Virgil's Messianic Eclogue but conveniently skipped the part of the prophecy about the way the Age would end in Fire  O Emperor  The World's Great Age begins anew  Our iron brood will cease and the Serpent die forever

as a new race of longhaired golden progeny descends from on high in Jefferson Airplanes
Oh Quaker King I hope you do not turn out still
to have the Jupiter Complex with the idea you can
win all war if you throw enough thunderbirds I
hope he's not you in disguise Old Nick  There's a
great Doomshape greybombhead in the sky Its

mouth is made of merde and it's saying Fuck You
to humanity and love The lights are burning late
in the Kremlin these nights trying to exorcise
that same Head which they see over them too A
huge paranoid vision of imagined hate + fear While
still in Moscow tonight there's music on Boro-
din Bridge and even tonight 'love slides down

50

the sides of the streets' 'Oh dreams of sweetness
of face Oh words like traces of love' 'We'll build
our new society on the vacant lots of the old'

Nixon oh Nixon I am not asking you to turn
and live with animals I am not asking you to commune
with trees although 'What times are these when a conver-

x

51

sation about a tree is almost a crime because it contains so many silences about so many crimes? I'm not asking you to squat and chant the Great Prajna Paramita Sutra although you might get high and learn Why Rivers Run Only One Way   It's an oriental secret which might give you a clue to the geo-politics of Vietnam  I'm not asking you to displace your Secondhand

God I'm not asking you to eat your figleaf  I'm just asking if you actually believe you can serve the people and the State at the same time or serve liberty and authority at the same time or tell the truth and lie with the same mouth  Will you ever invite the Living Theatre to your House  They might help you pretend to be yourself on TV  So lonely it hurts

Probably always a loner the kid on the block who always hung around the edges of the crowd wishing he
were the white-Haired Boy enrolled at Harvard at age
one Vice-Presidents are lonely and you were Vice-
Consul forever and probably all the time longing to be
loved by the same people who loved + hated Ken-
nedys Yes you're lonelier and stranger the longer

54

I look at you in all the disguises of your face
Stranger + stranger said Alice. Rosencrantz and
Guildenstern are both dead now and look who turns out
to be Hamming it  But let us pray the rest will
not be silence

Nixon oh Nixon when I saw you on TV last night

again stumbling through Vietnam you just didn't look like you believed who you were like as if it were all a strange mad dream you were lost in moving through the motions of some nightmare in which you suddenly found yourself in your pajamas in front of five million tea-ladies worried whether something was showing down there  Military might must be dis-

guised to be effective   It occurred to me your
warhead was showing My poet's shadow stit-
ched to thee won't stand many more such bull-
shit speeches   I had a weird feeling you
were speaking in a completely empty room Alone
with nothing but the War Machine like a toy behind
the pulpit   In another age you would have been

a Methodist preacher  In this one you're a real low priest  You're a true record of where winter is today

Nix oh Nix the original Fighting Quaker with your Wasp's nest on Plymouth Rock rigged with Pioneer Era Guidelines in a Great

Leap Backward into a new union-military-industrial
Dark Ages with far-out multi-media scenes of mass
paranoia as in Hieronymus Bosch death and sen-
suality wedded in buggering napalmed natives and/or
off-color students clitorises quivering in the ulti-
mate orgasm of death I salute thee national
pilot of our destinies in Air Force One I salute

thee mass murderer by complicity  While there is a
strung-out soul in Santa Rita Prison I am not free
While there is a napalmed class I am of it  I
raise my middle finger to you  smiling supporter of
benevolent imperial nationalism built upon political
falsehoods which still rule Washington DC and which you
and every other politician + president including Kennedy

were too political not to inherit   Don't call me
on your red telephone    War is good business
Invest your son
Nixon oh Nixon  I stayed up all night writing
this to thee and thine    I saw the dawn come up
over San Francisco   The Bay Bridge lights sparkled
in the first dawn  A dawn wind was rising   The guard

was changing in the Presidio mutiny stockade  Some.
where a Justice Department or FBI hi-fi repairman
was bugging a Berkeley Barb editor   At City Hall they
were celebrating the Nineteen-six Earthquake   Emperor Alioto and his Black Urban Affairs Director
whose name was actually Rebel were very much
in evidence but the evidence was all against a quake

It just wasn't going to happen here  No shake-
up here and no Revolution either and I have my
director to see to it  Souls on ice won't melt

Nixon! Nixon!  It was a long long night and now
I'm flying across the swinging rock face of this
America between the stiff wings of a metal bird

63

still writing to you although I have a weightless feeling

you're not giving me much attention Old Flappy Tongue

Give us some sign you hear us except that so

baleful simile of a smile    I'm not asking you

to solve my personal hangups or pathological problems

or I'll blow up the plane or take it to Cuba's

Territorio Libre though it might be a gas to let you out

at Havana Airport where you'd have to drink Cuba Libre
and look Fidel Castro in the eye and tell him without
benefit of electronic aides that your government does
not believe his truths while a lizard crawled out of
your eye      But our pilot now points out we're pass-
ing right over Rock Candy Mountain not too far from the
Great Salt Lake and I look down into the astonished

heart of North America in the first blink of light  It occurs
to me you've flown this route so often you don't even look
down anymore at the great hard sweet tit of America
above which tyrant birds still catch their prey on the wing
and I hope you're not one of that still-extant species  Your
land is my land but the cleavage down there is too great to be
sexy and the Golden Spike was driven by Chinks  We wouldn't

want you to fall into the sweet-and-sour sauce
We won't put rock salt on your tail yet But hurry hurry
we can't hold our breath forever We don't have to
accept forever the pornofacts of Death

O Nixon Nixon I've cycled through your America
and through my America    I have seen the faces

Let us now praise unfamous men  The People Yes
and No  including Indian chiefs and tyrants queers
Kings hausfraus athletes parents policemen bosses
soldiers sex-offenders jewish newspapermen longhaired students and Tuli Kupferberg  I see
we're all demented remnants of light and
ecstasy Derelicts in time trying to reconstruct

with only faint recall a lost message Peace Music
Love Revolution Joy     This is the first day of the
rest of your life    This is your Safe Conduct Pass
There is Nothing to fear     For Nothing is the
only thing to fear    And Nothing the only thing
to fear in a face     I've hitched back and
forth across the face of America looking for

a face    I once rode a freight from Joplin
to Chattanooga  and saw your face on a siding
It was the face of the Yard Dick busting the
sterno bums   I was a college kid and
thought it was fun   The whole world a frater-
nity razing   But now I remember the face
in the dark by the tracks the dark jowls and

the hard eyes like yours oh American Dick  The
Eagle flies today brandishing olive branches and thunder-
bolts  Which will you drop on us  Nixon oh Nixon

now is the time for the seventh-inning stretch  So
let us still hope there'll be some joy in Mudville tonight

Walk softly and carry a big wick to light the lights of

the world   For the river of light is within us   Walk

softly and bury the Big Stick for the World might still

end in a Freudian slip   oh Slippery Dick oh goy Golem

of all our dreams   This really isn't addressed to

you   It's a curse and a cry to any old President

or any old general or any assassin or lover

who happens to be running things by the time this is printed    So good luck Golem of all our days I have nothing more to lay on you unless you have something more + different to say to me    Good luck sweet rockcandy dreams to you + yours    You might yet learn to unmask your Self    You might yet move the magic moloch mountain with its misplaced Eye

The Lotus might yet open and open into the very stoned

heart of light   The void of serenity might yet prove

not too strange for the mind of man   We are daily

faced with the Miraculous   And the air is electric

with hate   And the air is alive with love

and we are charged with loving You too

# NOTES

to allege various thefts and plunderings:

Page 1   'populist hymn': echoes Vachel Lindsay's 'Bryan
Bryan Bryan'. A Bryan-Nixon parallel is incidentally
obnoxious. As far back as Populism, America was already
seen as an 'empire dealing with its own minorities
as it deals with its client-states overseas.' (cf. John
McDermott reviewing 'The Agony of the American Left'
in The Nation, June 23, 1969)

Page 1   'our history is noble and tragic like the mask of
a tyrant': Apollinaire, AL COOLS.

Page 1  'the mask an actor wears is apt to become his face':
cf. TDR (The Drama Review) issue on the Living Theatre,
Spring, 1969.

Page 8  'manunkind': e.e. cummings' 'pity this busy
monster manunkind'.

Page 19  'The War Against Youth': Senator George Mc-
Govern in a speech at Aberdeen, S.D. (San Francisco Chronicle, May 30, 1969).

Page 19  'people a danger to the public': Bertolt Brecht.

Page 19  'trans-ceiver mechanisms': cf. Buckminster Fuller,
No More Secondhand God.

Page 20 'probably only someone fiddling with his moustache in a hopeless cellar': Allen Ginsberg in conversation with Dostoevsky.

Page 20 'The American Dream doesn't come...': Nixon Inaugural speech.

Page 21 'riders on the earth together': Archibald Macleish

Page 22 'Love the fourth position': Cf. Thomas A. Harris, I'm OK, You're OK (Harper, 1969)

Page 23 'Uncle Ahab': Uncle Sam — Captain Ahab. Cf. Moby Dick : 'Oh! Ahab,' cried Starbuck, 'not too late is it, even now, the third day, to desist. See! Moby Dick seeks thee not. It is thou,

thou, thou madly seekest him!"'

Page 23 'voyaging continually abroad...': George Kennan
on U.S. foreign policy during Johnson error [SIC].

Page 24 'yellow submarine': the Beatles' boat.

Page 24 'Life flows on...etc': Beatles LP 'Sergeant Pepper.'

Page 25 'Green Flag': first raised at People's Park, Berkeley, May, 1969, alongside the black and red flags
of anarchy and revolution. (Cf. Green Flag, Journal
for the Protection of All Beings, #3, City Lights
Books, June, 1969.)

Page 26 'real man or real machine': Norman Mailer in
Miami and the Siege of Chicago.

Page 27 'nazification': the San Francisco Chronicle, not generally known as an Underground paper, carried the following phrases either editorially or in news stories on May 29, 1969: 'Yahoos governing California,' 'Nazification of Berkeley,' 'New McCarthy Era.'

Page 27 'one of us': James Rector, 25-year-old 'Non-student' shot down by an officer of the Alameda County sheriff's department, in Berkeley, May, 1969.

Page 29 'with the same sponsor': this is not a poetic fiction. A domestic manufacturer of war matériel is as much a sponsor of war as he is of the domestic product he sponsors on TV. There are plenty of examples. 'Their product is death, their market is war.' (Cf. 'Plain Rapper' published by Palo Alto Resistance, esp. April-May, 1969).

Pages 32-33 'Don't wear sandals Avoid scandal': Bob Dylan.

Pages 33-34 'Nixon Nixon burning bright': Blake's Tyger. 'And will the Lamb follow you': Will Vice-President Agnew (whose name means Lamb in French: <u>agneau</u>) succeed the Lionhearted as President. Etc, etc. Help.

Page 35 'Frozen soul of America who will cling to the wreckage': Variation of a line in Daniel Moore's Floating Lotus Opera, #3, (Berkeley, summer, 1969).

Page 38 'grant the Serpent free Speech': from a poem by Richard
        Ogar, Berkeley, June, 1969.
Page 40 'Let us eat light': when asked how she subsisted
        on only a wafer a day, Theresa Neumann replied
        'I live on God's light.' Baba Ram Das (Richard Alpert)
        quoted her in a talk on 'Yoga, higher consciousness,
        psychedelics, psychology, and the Western scene'
        in San Francisco, June, 1969. Only he said she said
        'I ate light.' God got lost in the expansion of consciousness.
Page 40 'pickpocket who meets a saint': Baba Rama Das, same talk.
Page 40 'a man who picks you up hitchhiking in a sunny central
        spot...etc': Richard Berman in conversation at City Lights.

Page 44 'the poets in their sad likenesses': Many American poets
do in fact help the Government in maintaining a <u>status
quo</u> which is supported by and supports War as
a legal form of murder: witness the number
of avant-garde poets and Little Presses who
have in recent years accepted U.S. grants directly
from the National Foundation on the Arts or from
its conduit, the Coordinating Council of Literary
Magazines, making it clear the avant-garde in the
arts is not <u>necessarily</u> to be associated with the
political Left. Cf. Marcuse's 'repressive tolerance'
i.e., the policy of tolerance and/or sponsorship

as a self-protection against violence; or as Susan Sontag
recently put it, 'divesting unsettling or subversive ideas
by ingesting them.'    (Ramparts, June, 1969).

Page 44 'Open the door to a room with a lot of other doors':
White House press aide commenting on Nixon Vietnam speech.
No doors were seen to open. Back-door diplomacy, perhaps.

Page 44 'Doors of Perception': cf. Huxley and Blake, of course.

Page 45 'addicted to that inner place': Baba Ram Das, op. cit.

Page 48 'whoever wrote our dollar bill': the Latin on our bill
comes from Virgil's Fourth Eclogue which begins:

'Ultima Cumaei venit iam carminis aetas;
magnus ab integro saeclorum nascitur ordo.

iam redit et Virgo, redeunt Saturnia regna;
iam nova progenies caelo demittitur alto.
tu modo nascenti puero, quo ferrea primum
desinet ac toto surget gens aurea mundo,
casta fave Lucina: tuus iam regnat Apollo.'
Adaptation of Loeb Classics translation:
'Now is come the last age of Cumaean Song;
the great circuit of the centuries begins anew.
Now the virgin returns, Saturn's reign returns;
now a new generation descends from on high.
Only smile, pure Lucina, on the birth of the child,
under whom the iron brood shall first cease,

and a golden race spring up throughout the world.
Thine own Apollo now is king.' (Prophecy
not only of the coming of Christ on earth but of
spacecraft Apollo.)

Page 48 'the wind still whispered Latin phrases': variation
of a line in Apollinaire, ALCOOLS.

Pages 50-51 'love slides down the sides of the streets'
'oh dreams of sweetness...etc': the fact
that these phrases come from a contemporary
Cuban poet emphasizes the point: Nancy
Morejón in <u>Con Cuba</u>, translated by Tim Reynolds.

Page 51 'We'll build our new society on the vacant lots of the old": from a speech by Wendy Schlessinger of the People's Park Negotiating Committee, Berkeley, May, 1969.

Page 51 'turn and live with animals': Whitman.

Pages 51-52 'what times are these': entire quote from Bertolt Brecht (translation: Reinhard Lettau).

Page 53 'serve the people and the state at the same time': Cf. TDR issue on The Living Theatre. See also Marcuse, Eros and Civilization re. the virtual impossibility of a 'non-repressive society.'

Page 53 'pretend to be yourself': Living Theatre, op.cit.

Page 55 'Rosencrantz and Guildenstern': despite the fact they are obviously Jewish, R+G may now be seen

to have had something in common with the murdered
Kennedy brothers, folk heroes and dupes of fate,
destroyed by forces they set out to destroy.
In the contemporary play, "Rosencrantz and Guilden-
stern Are Dead" they are martyrs not villains.
Page 55 "Hamming it... the rest will not be silence":
Hamlet, of course. Gregory Corso showed himself
a prophet almost ten years ago in a poem called
"America Politica Historia, In Spontaneity":
        "Nixon arrives ever so temporal, self-made,
        frontways sideways and backways
        could he be America's against? Detour to vehicle?

mast to wind? shore to sea? Death to life?
The last President?' (Chelsea Review, Oct, 1960)

Page 58 'Pioneer Era Guidelines', 'Great Leap Backward':
cf. The Moomaw Report, guidelines for schools
prepared by Rev. Donn Moomaw, Governor Reagan's pastor.

Page 58 'Wasp's nest': white Anglo Saxon Protestant.

Page 60 'While there is a strung-out soul in Santa Rita':
Cf. Eugene Debs: 'While there is a lower class
I am in it; while there is a soul in prison I am
not free...' Santa Rita is infamous as the
prison to which hundreds of Berkeley demonstrators
were sent in May '69. The author spent some time

there on an earlier Peace bust. (Ramparts, March '68)

Page 61 'War is good business Invest your son': Bumpersticker.

Page 62 'Emperor Alioto': not necessarily an insult to the
Mayor of San francisco. He's got style. A Sicilian
Anarchist poet named Buttitta, 88 years old, told
me in Sicily last year that the name Alioto is a
corruption of a prominent Mafia name in the
mother country. No one is saying our Mayor is Mafia.
I am merely reporting hearsay etymology.

Page 63 'souls on ice': Cf. Eldridge Cleaver.

Page 66 'tyrant birds': Cf. Webster: Tyrannidae.

Page 67 'the pornofacts of death': Cf. a speech by Professor

Pages 68-69    George Wald, 'The Facts of Death' (1969).
'demented remnants', 'derelicts in time
trying to reconstruct' etc: R.D. Laing,
<u>The Politics of Experience</u>.

Page 69    'This is the first day of the rest of your
life': Bumpersticker.

Page 69    'There is *Nothing* to fear': R.D. Laing, op.cit.

Page 71    'The Eagle flies today': See our Great Seal
again: the dollar bill: in the Left claw of the
Eagle an olive branch; in the Right, thun-
derbolts. (Left becomes Right when viewed
from behind.)

Page 71 'joy in Mudville': Cf. 'Casey at the Bat.'
Page 71 'the river of light is within us': Daniel Moore,
    Floating Lotus.
Page 72 'a goy Golem':
    goy: a Gentile; someone dull + insensitive.
    golem: from Hebrew: matter without shape.
    'A robot, a lifeless figure, a simpleton,
    a fool, a clumsy man or woman, a clod,
    someone all thumbs, poorly co-ordinated;
    a graceless, tactless type; someone
    subnormal. 'A Golem can be virtuous, kind,

just, said Maimonides, but his intellectual capacities are limited." (Leo Rosten, _The Joys of Yiddish_, McGraw Hill, 1968).

Page 74 'void of serenity': This is an answer to the question posed by Daniel Moore in the Floating Lotus Opera: "Is the void of serenity too strange for the mind of man?" I have stolen his phrases in toto. He's the greater poet, I the better 'craftsman.' [SIC: Ezra Pound]

Unsorted pop notes: Jefferson Airplane: San Francisco rock group.

Rig + wick: genitalia (Cf. Rolling Stone, Feb. 15, 1969).